THE DELEGATION PO

By Dr. Jon Warner

Drawings by Phil Hailstone

"Delegation has always been a bit of a 'hit or miss' affair for me in the past but this pocketbook has given me a much better appreciation not only of what I should be doing but also how. I have already started to see better outcomes as a result."
Helen Lewis, HR Director, Healthnet

"Finding the time to delegate has always been a big personal challenge. However, after carrying out several of the exercises and suggestions in this book, I quickly realised that over half of what I was doing could be done by others. This has helped me make much more effective use of my time."
Sue Casanovas, Training Manager, Kingston Hospital NHS Trust

Published by:
Management Pocketbooks Ltd
Laurel House, Station Approach, Alresford, Hants SO24 9JH, U.K.
Tel: +44 (0)1962 735573 Fax: +44 (0)1962 733637
E-mail: sales@pocketbook.co.uk
Website: www.pocketbook.co.uk

This edition published 2008.

British Library Cataloguing-in-Publication Data – A catalogue record for this book is available from the British Library.

ISBN 978 1 903776 91 9

Design, typesetting and graphics by **efex ltd**. Printed in U.K.

CONTENTS

INTRODUCTION

AN ESSENTIAL TOOL

If every person had sufficient time, energy and ability they could, quite possibly, do everything themselves. In such circumstances there would be little need for teams, for people to work together or to share workload. The need to delegate would not exist.

The typical manager, however, tends to be time-starved and overloaded with work, frequently lacking the knowledge or experience to perform every task equally well. As a result, delegation is an essential tool in the manager's toolkit, and one worth using in the best way possible.

This pocketbook, therefore, aims to offer you some broad guidance, as well as a mixture of ideas, tools and methods to help you to delegate more successfully in the future.

INTRODUCTION

GOOD & BAD DELEGATION

At face value at least, delegating a task or project should be relatively straightforward. You simply assign a task to a given individual or team, agree on milestones and some kind of measurement system, monitor progress and, finally, offer feedback to the individual when the task is complete. However, the ways in which you engage with people in each of these four steps can be quite different.

There is also, of course, a big difference between good and bad delegation.

Good delegation saves you time, develops people, helps to build skills (or even groom a successor), and is motivating.

Bad delegation causes you frustration, demotivates and confuses the other person, and fails to achieve the task or purpose itself.

Delegation is a management skill that can be used more. Time spent on improving your ability to delegate well will reap reward later on.

SHOULD YOU DELEGATE?

QUESTIONNAIRE

How ready are you to delegate? Identify how many of the questions below apply to you.

- Do you work longer hours than you should? ◯
- Do you often feel exhausted by the sheer volume of work that you have? ◯
- Do you have unfinished jobs mounting up that you are unable to clear? ◯
- Do you spend time doing things for others that they could do themselves? ◯
- Do you struggle to meet deadlines? ◯
- Do you often fall behind on projects and have to work uncomfortably hard to catch up? ◯
- Do you find yourself working on details rather than the bigger picture? ◯
- Do you do particular jobs because you enjoy them, not because you need to? ◯
- Do you hang on to work because you want to keep control? ◯
- Do you lack confidence in others to do a good job? ◯

If you answered yes to 3 or more of these 10 questions, then you have opportunities to delegate much more than you do at the moment. If you answered yes to 7 or more of these questions, this book will offer you several new ideas to try.

UNDERSTANDING DELEGATION

DEFINING DELEGATION

The dictionary defines delegation as:

Delegation
Entrusting an individual or individuals to take on a particular work task(s) or to make certain decisions

We will explore the usefulness of this definition in the course of this book. To begin with, let's look at two ways in which this process of 'entrusting' can occur – formal and informal.

FORMAL OR INFORMAL?

In a **formal structure**, delegation may occur as part of the manager/subordinate relationship (with the manager offering direct instructions on how tasks should be broken up and who should do them).

If a broadly-based system of seniority also operates, tasks may be delegated according to grade or status, with the more junior people taking on the 'doing tasks' and their seniors responsible for the thinking or planning.

FORMAL OR INFORMAL?

In an **informal structure**, delegation does not follow a system of seniority and it can sometimes be possible for an individual to delegate tasks to colleagues, helping them out in return on some other task.

In an informal process, with no fixed authority structure to dictate procedure, people may spend more time discussing options and choices about what is done, how it is done and who does it. In other words, as you understand the **capacity, capabilities** and **competencies** of the people around you, reciprocal delegation opportunities start to appear – you help some people and they, in turn, help you. This assists you in achieving the overall objectives of the organisation more successfully and helps to bring about better team work at all levels.

HOW MUCH DELEGATION?

It is almost certain that, at some time or another, you will have had to ask others for assistance. This could vary from them taking messages or phone calls to deputising at a meeting, or even to handling quite a large or complex project for you. By asking someone to help you, you've delegated part of your job. So, if you can delegate (even in a minor way) on occasions such as this, or when you go on holiday or are away from work for any reason, why can't you do it more often?

The aim of this book is to help make delegation part of your normal work schedule, and to identify occasions when you can help others (when they delegate to you because you have greater skills or capacity) and occasions when you can entrust other people with delegated tasks (because they have the capability to help you and to grow from the experience).

HOW YOU SEE IT

It is helpful to think carefully about your attitude to the whole process of delegation. Start by rating each statement in the simple questionnaire shown below and use the 1-5 scale to see where you stand.

Statement	1 (Agree)	2	3	4	5 (Disagree)
1. Supervisors/managers should be able to do the jobs of each of their subordinates to at least the same standard.	1	2	3	4	5
2. A manager should always be on hand to sort things out.	1	2	3	4	5
3. A manager should be seen to be busy at all times.	1	2	3	4	5
4. If managers let their subordinates make more decisions, it weakens their control and authority.	1	2	3	4	5
5. If you want something done properly you have to do it yourself.	1	2	3	4	5
6. Unless subordinates are performing well in their own job, a manager should not delegate to them.	1	2	3	4	5

HOW YOU SEE IT

		1 Agree	2	3	4	5 Disagree
7.	Subordinates should always have the limits of their authority clearly defined.	1	2	3	4	5
8.	The main reason why managers shouldn't delegate is because you can't really trust subordinates.	1	2	3	4	5
9.	Delegation is an 'art' and as such only a few managers actually practise it.	1	2	3	4	5
10.	Delegation is simply about telling people exactly what you want, then leaving them to get on with it.	1	2	3	4	5

So, how many of these questions did you give a maximum 5 to?

Typically, the most effective delegators strongly disagree with all these statements. If this is not the case for you, you may want to think more deeply about your willingness to delegate and what it will take to change your view.

BARRIERS TO EFFECTIVE DELEGATION

Most people will have one or two particular blocks or barriers that they can't seem to overcome when they even think about delegating work.

These could be worries about the extra time that delegation will take, the effort and skill required to explain a project, a lack of confidence in self or others, or even the worry that the person being delegated to might actually do the job better. Whatever the reason, these barriers need to be identified and challenged.

Try engaging for a few minutes in this simple personal reflection activity:

- Think back to yesterday, or a day earlier in the week if you prefer, and jot down all that you did, in no particular order.
- Now examine that list and ask yourself if others could have done some of those jobs instead of you?
- What stopped you asking others for help?

COST OF NOT LETTING GO

While not letting go may sometimes be a deliberate choice, such choices do not come without a cost. By failing to delegate, real and tangible costs may be incurred in terms of inefficiency and poor productivity. In addition, you will probably be paying a high personal price:

- Working far too many hours (bad for your long-term health)
- Concentrating on the wrong priorities
- Too busy to develop any new skills
- Missing important deadlines
- Seeing the quality of your work suffer

You are also denying others opportunities to:

- Develop their skills
- Realise their potential
- Increase their job satisfaction

DELEGATING FOR THE WRONG REASONS

Delegation is not always the solution and it can be used for entirely the wrong reasons. These include:

- Disliking your work (and delegating to get out of it)
- Being unable to do your job properly (and hoping someone else will rescue you)
- Penalising someone you don't like
- Sheer laziness or lack of commitment

Delegating for any of these reasons will foster distrust and lead to people feeling put upon or taken advantage of. They won't take on future legitimate delegation tasks willingly or with much motivation to do the job well. It is important to get the balance right.

BEING TOO TENTATIVE

Being tentative about delegating and too concerned about an individual's ability to perform a task that you genuinely wish to delegate will do little to set the process off on the right track.

You will greatly enhance people's confidence if you are able to give them tasks with your full trust and belief in their ability to complete them successfully.

For individuals to feel properly motivated, they need to perceive that the climate is liberating rather than constraining. In other words, they need to feel that the delegator is confident about their ability not only to do the task, but to do it (at least to some extent) in their own way, without being over prescriptive. **This is often called specifying the 'what' but not the 'how'**.

Before you look at the next page, you may want to take a moment to list any reasons you still have for NOT delegating.

REASONS FOR NOT DELEGATING

How many of the following are still on your list?

- You like to maintain the impression of being overworked
- Too much to do – you cannot make the time/effort to delegate
- Enjoying the job so much that it's difficult to let go
- Believing you're indispensable
- Lack of trust in others
- Fear of losing your job or being replaced
- Fear of losing face
- Imposing unnecessarily high standards
- Concern at overloading other people
- Fear of criticism

Hopefully, we have already helped you to cross a few of these reasons off your list and you are ready to start delegating more often. Perhaps, by now looking at the many benefits of delegating, we can remove all the remaining barriers.

BENEFITS OF DELEGATION

Once you have accepted that many of the common barriers to delegation are more about your own limiting attitudes than anything else, you can start to appreciate the many advantages it offers, both to you personally and to others.

The following are just a few ideas on how delegation can benefit you personally as a delegator. Try to add to this list.

By delegating you are:

- Freeing yourself up to do the more important jobs on your schedule
- Developing the skills of others
- Making jobs more interesting
- Giving tasks to people who may be more skilled at particular aspects than you
- Demonstrating confidence in others
- Giving people room to try new things and grow

STRIKING THE RIGHT BALANCE

Many people find it very difficult to let go, no matter how much they understand about the theory of delegation or how much training they receive. Such people tend to be at one end or other of the personal organisation scale, either highly organised or highly disorganised. On the next page is a simple diagram that indicates this scale on a see-saw with 'balance', in the centre, the ideal approach.

Getting the balance right requires you to find a happy medium between over-delegation and under-delegation. **Over-delegation** means dumping work, knowingly giving a person a lot more than he or she is likely to be able to handle in the time involved. This is a gross distortion of the entire process and philosophy of delegation.

If someone is **under-delegating**, the individual taking on the work is likely to feel that he or she has been given too little control, and will become frustrated. Alternatively, they may feel willing and able to take more on, but inhibited from doing so.

To delegate in a balanced way, the delegator should always ensure that the other person has the ability to comment on the plan before any work is started.

THE DELEGATION SEE-SAW

Highly organised person

Often under-delegates by taking on most tasks by themselves, offering no project work, coaching or development to others.

Needs to use their organisational skills to organise others to take on tasks and projects.

Needs to spend quality time helping others to understand their goals and deadlines to bring more order into their work.

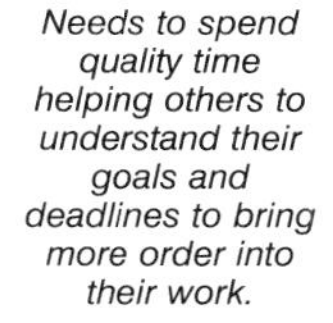

Highly disorganised person

Often over-delegates to others, causing missed deadlines, confusion and frustration at the lack of control.

BALANCE

Achieving the right delegation balance

THE DELEGATION SEE-SAW

HIGHLY DISORGANISED

The highly disorganised person, at one end of the see-saw, is always looking for that elusive report, phone number or notes from the meeting: *'I had it a moment ago'* being a typical excuse. They are often late for meetings and might meet deadlines only by the skin of their teeth.

Unfortunately these people rarely have the time or capacity to get themselves organised in order to help others. The irony is that they are the very people who ought to start letting go and involving others. Sadly, when they do, they often lack the credibility – and skills – to come across as plausible.

THE DELEGATION SEE-SAW

HIGHLY ORGANISED

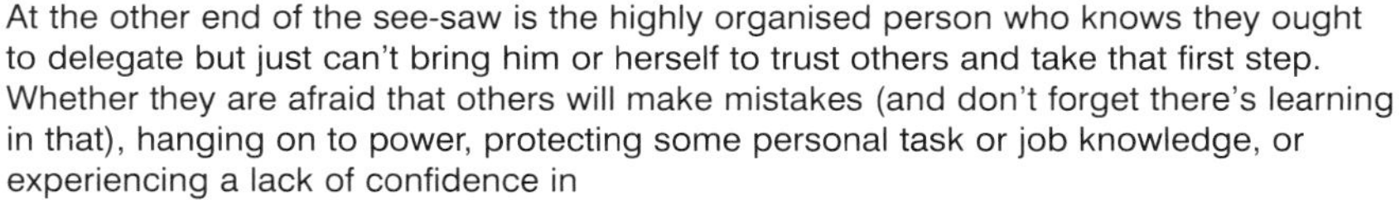

At the other end of the see-saw is the highly organised person who knows they ought to delegate but just can't bring him or herself to trust others and take that first step. Whether they are afraid that others will make mistakes (and don't forget there's learning in that), hanging on to power, protecting some personal task or job knowledge, or experiencing a lack of confidence in themselves or others, delegation just doesn't happen.

So where would you put yourself – somewhere between the two? With help, and by developing some new perspectives on the subject (as well as a few new skills), perhaps you could let go more often.

HOW OTHERS CAN BENEFIT

For other people delegation can mean:

- The chance to do things they wouldn't normally do
- Taking on new skills and responsibilities
- The opportunity to work with new and different people
- The chance to prove themselves
- Training in new skills
- Job enrichment or job enlargement

Hence, both the delegator and those to whom the work is delegated can achieve a 'win/win' outcome. This is particularly the case, of course, if delegation occurs in a positive and empowering way.

THE DELEGATION PROCESS

5 STAGE SEQUENCE

Having looked at what delegation involves, the barriers to engaging in it and the potential advantages, let's consider in more detail how the process should work sequentially. Although there is no one formula for delegation, a simple 5 stage sequence can be followed:

1. Identify the task/project
Look in detail at your priorities. Identify things that others could do or help you with.

2. Identify the right person
Who could help you? Are they willing, capable and interested? Think about workload and timing issues.

3. Brief the person and set goals and priorities
Discuss what you're aiming for and by when. Set specific goals/targets and invite questions.

4. Support the individual appropriately
Offer help in the form of coaching, training and/or appropriate support. Set review milestones and monitor progess.

5. Recognise the effort or contribution
Offer positive recognition. Learn jointly from the experience for next time.

1: IDENTIFY THE TASK/PROJECT

GENERAL AREAS FOR DELEGATION

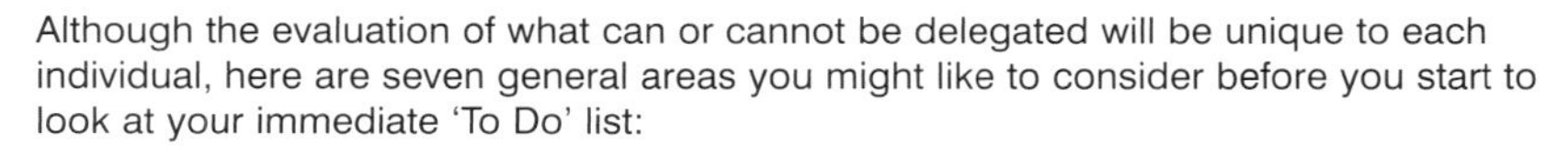

Although the evaluation of what can or cannot be delegated will be unique to each individual, here are seven general areas you might like to consider before you start to look at your immediate 'To Do' list:

- Repetitive or routine tasks or actions that you perform frequently
- Technical work that others are better equipped to handle
- Immediate opportunities for direct reports or colleagues to work together
- Work that will increase the experience and/or skill of direct reports or colleagues
- Opportunities to 'unleash' individual creativity
- Any tasks or projects that will provide job-enrichment or variety for others
- Tasks or actions that will increase the breadth of responsibility of direct reports or colleagues

1: IDENTIFY THE TASK/PROJECT

SELECTING THE RIGHT TASK(S)

The ideal place to start, when looking to delegate work, is to think about what tangible outcomes you have to achieve within the next day, week or, even, month. This will help you to consider what tasks or projects are likely to be suitable for delegation and then to break them down into smaller tasks that may lend themselves to spreading the load.

For example, a manager juggling with several priorities, with insufficient time to complete all of them by a deadline (or to an appropriate quality standard), should review which tasks seem best suited to delegation, whether as a whole or in part.

THE DELEGATION PROCESS

1: IDENTIFY THE TASK/PROJECT

REMEMBER TIME MANAGEMENT PRINCIPLES

It is always important to spend enough time preparing and being as organised as possible (don't just off-load work to others in an attempt to lighten your load). Put simply, this means using the familiar time management principles of:

- Creating a weekly plan of jobs you have to do
- Translating these into daily 'To Do' lists (which we will look at next)
- Categorising tasks into urgent and important (or both) and prioritising them
- Applying the Pareto principle as much as you can (20% of the tasks you do will lead to 80% of the results)
- Grouping related activities together to concentrate your efforts
- Being realistic (there's only so much you can do)

THE DELEGATION PROCESS

1: IDENTIFY THE TASK/PROJECT

REVIEW YOUR 'TO DO' LIST

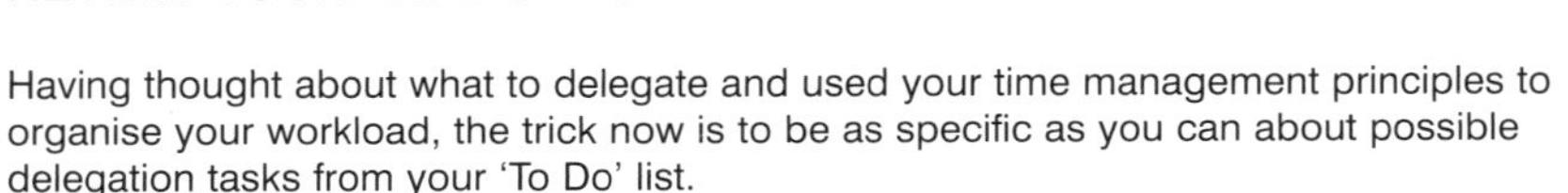

Having thought about what to delegate and used your time management principles to organise your workload, the trick now is to be as specific as you can about possible delegation tasks from your 'To Do' list.

The following are broad examples of what you might usefully delegate:

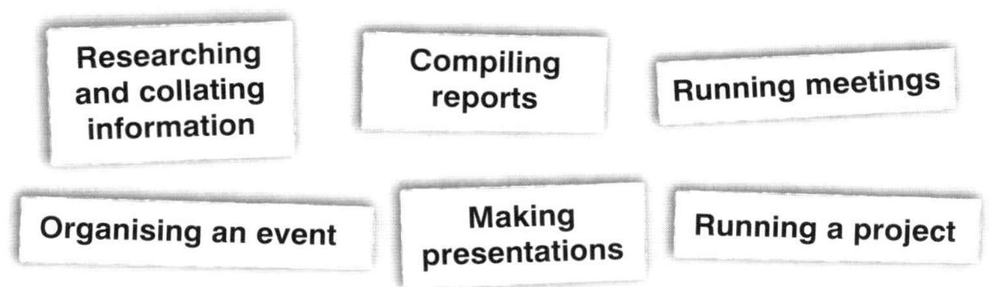

You now need to be much more specific about the benefits that delegation will bring to you and to others. You will need to draw upon this when you get to the briefing stage.

1: IDENTIFY THE TASK/PROJECT

LOOK FOR SUBSTANTIAL TASKS

Simply asking someone to photocopy some papers, send an email on your behalf or make a phone call, is hardly going to tax their abilities, although it may help you out. What's more, they are unlikely to learn much in the process.

When choosing jobs to delegate, look for:

- Tasks that others could do quicker, better or cheaper than you
- Routine jobs and associated decision-making
- Complete jobs that will give a sense of satisfaction (even better if there is some scope for the individual to use their own initiative – rather than simply following a set routine)
- Jobs that require expertise: if someone is better qualified to do it than you, then ask them

2: IDENTIFY THE RIGHT PERSON

THE WIIFM FACTOR

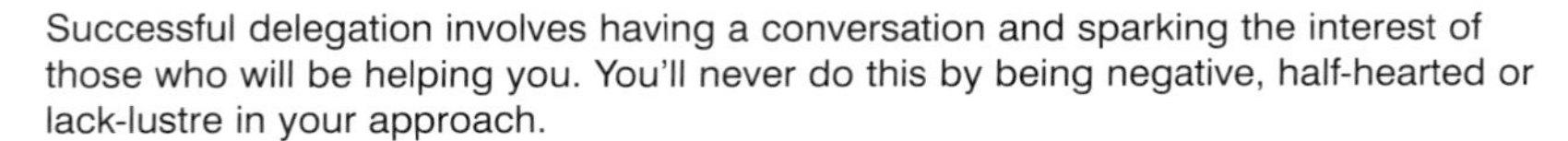
Successful delegation involves having a conversation and sparking the interest of those who will be helping you. You'll never do this by being negative, half-hearted or lack-lustre in your approach.

Always bear in mind the WIIFM factor (*What's In It For Me*) that is often uppermost in people's minds, and try to view delegation from the other person's point of view. The more the person to whom you are delegating genuinely wants to do the task, the better. This is why, when identifying the right task, you need to be specific about the benefits so that you can now describe them in terms that are attractive to the person undertaking the work.

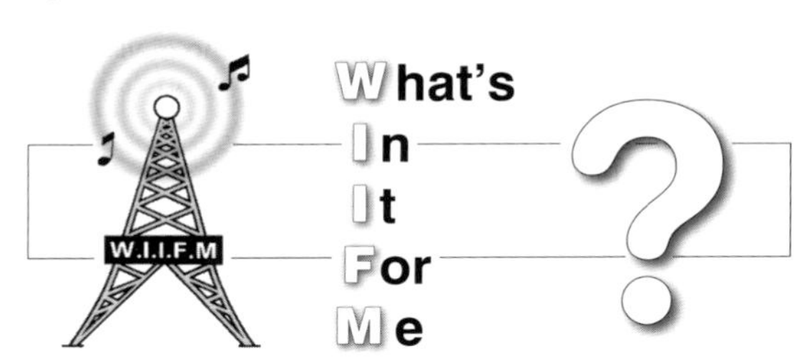

2: IDENTIFY THE RIGHT PERSON

ASSESSING CAPABILITIES

Having identified the most suitable tasks to delegate, and considered the benefits for any individual taking them on, you can start to think about who is best suited to help. Of course, the person needs to have sufficient time to spare. But this aside, you need some method for assessing their capabilities. (Remember that you can offer to trade with them and take work off their hands at a later date, in return.)

One way to think about your team members or colleagues differently, with a view to delegation, is to draw up a simple table such as the one shown on the next page.

2: IDENTIFY THE RIGHT PERSON

SKILLS MATRIX

	Skill Set 1	Skill Set 2	Skill Set 3	Skill Set 4
Ahmed	Making presentations	Meeting management		
Mary	Spreadsheets	Databases		
Joel	Teambuilding			
Liz	Conflict resolution	Negotiating	Report writing	Making presentations
Carole	Budgeting			

In using such a table, each skill is listed in priority order (according to its perceived strength). Note also that individuals may have the same skills (like Ahmed and Liz) but not necessarily at the same level.

2: IDENTIFY THE RIGHT PERSON

GIVE ENCOURAGEMENT

If the individual feels capable of the task, he or she should always be encouraged to take it on (even if it is a bit outside their normal range). The chance to learn new skills should not be turned down, and if the person acquits themselves well, it will be of benefit to both parties.

If an individual seems to have the right skill set to undertake a delegated task, you will need to ensure that he or she also has the **authority** to do the work. This means that if you ask someone to do something, you also give him or her the power and the freedom to do it. This often simply requires letting others know that the person is now responsible and in charge of the particular project outcomes, thus giving them public authority and encouragement from the outset.

3: BRIEFING & GOAL SETTING

We will look at the communication process in more depth later in this book. In summary, however, once you have selected the person to whom you wish to delegate, you need to carefully discuss what you are aiming for in giving them the task in question. In particular you need to review together the **specific goals and targets**. This allows the person to ask questions and for you to offer any help necessary in clarifying the task.

Being clear about the task's aims and priorities will ensure that people ultimately meet your standards and do what you want them to do. In addition, you may need to adopt a particular briefing style.

The delegator's prime task when briefing others is to communicate in language that is simple, concise, to the point and helps to bring about full or complete understanding of the task.

3: BRIEFING & GOAL SETTING

DELEGATION OR ABDICATION

There's a major difference between delegation and abdication or abrogation – the latter meaning that you give up all responsibility for your personal accountabilities. Clearly, if you simply hand over a job, indicating that you are fed up or can't be bothered, it's hardly going to inspire someone to give of their best.

When delegating, you should always retain overall responsibility, and make this clear to the person undertaking the work.

The chart on the next page is a good way to think about how to separate what you must do or hold onto at the core from less essential tasks.

3: BRIEFING & GOAL SETTING

THE DELEGATION ONION

Try thinking about your tasks in terms of the layers of an onion, as shown in the diagram.

Just like the onion, the core is the most important part which you should keep to yourself and control personally. For the outer, more disposable, layers you can involve others and use delegation increasingly.

4: APPROPRIATE SUPPORT

There is obviously a huge difference between delegating a small job (eg a few phone calls) and a large task or project (eg preparing for and giving a major presentation to senior management on your behalf). As a result, the need for help and support will vary greatly according to both the complexities of the task and the experience and general needs of the person to whom you are delegating. However, in both cases, support should always be available to the individual and it is he or she who should determine how much help they may require.

Some experienced, knowledgeable or confident individuals may be happy just to get on with it, while others may require a lot of support (including some relevant training and ongoing coaching). Don't forget, the delegator's job is to 'keep a watchful brief' as the individual undertakes the task, so as to be there when needed.

4: APPROPRIATE SUPPORT

SETTING MILESTONES

One of the ways support can be offered to individuals on more or less all delegated tasks is to jointly set review milestones and monitor progress according to what was agreed.

For a small or minor task you may only need one or two milestones (eg in the middle of the task and near completion). The monitoring will take the form of a brief conversation to discuss any matters which have not gone exactly according to plan. However, for more complex tasks/projects that will take longer to complete, many review milestones will be necessary, and the monitoring process may be correspondingly more involved (including, for example, weekly meetings, statistical reporting and submitting written notes).

Once again, the individual to whom the work is delegated is in the best position to drive the review and monitoring process. As the person ultimately responsible for the task, however, you also have to be comfortable that the monitoring system will allow you to intervene constructively, should your help or support be needed to get things back on track.

5: RECOGNISE THE EFFORT

Even managers who start off quite reluctant to delegate can, with increased practice and experience, become almost blasé about the process, and forget to review events with the individual at the end. This is particularly the case when tasks are short or apparently straightforward, or if the person doing the task is reliable and regularly achieves good results.

Managers should therefore make a special effort to recognise the effort and contribution made in every instance of delegation. This should occur even when the task was achieved simply and unremarkably but especially when there were difficult issues to be overcome. This allows both parties to sign off on the task properly and to draw out any learning (for both parties) that came out of the experience.

5: RECOGNISE THE EFFORT

Having recognised WIIFM factors when first delegating the task, you need to give just as much motivation and encouragement at the end. This is because delegation is a **voluntary** agreement between manager and individual. The manager offers work that needs to be done but should help the person to learn and grow. Reciprocally, the individual takes on the work in the knowledge that it will require extra time but provides an opportunity to increase skills and experience, sometimes in completely new areas.

This voluntary exchange 'contract' can be repeated in the future but it will often only be entered into if the manager tangibly recognises the effort and contribution made by the individual each time. As well as achieving the immediately beneficial outcome of making the individual feel that the manager is interested and grateful, this serves to signal to the person and other colleagues on the team that delegation work is worth undertaking.

CASE STUDY: JENNIFER'S CHALLENGE

The case study on the following pages gives you the opportunity to review the process of choosing the right tasks to delegate. Try to develop an appropriate delegation strategy – what would you do if you were in Jennifer's position?

With the Christmas break only two weeks away, Jennifer looked at her To Do list and shook her head. If she ignored the minor items, she had ten major priorities to complete before the end of the year. Even with no interruptions or other pressing matters, she would be lucky to get half of them done.

TO DO List

1. Phil's appraisal discussion.
2. Visit the office furniture supplier.
3. Proof read 80-page report for typos and mistakes.
4. Organise the joint department training course for the beginning of January.
5. Plan the office relocation to another floor.
6. Prioritise last month's customer complaints for action follow-up.
7. Call the team together to talk through next year's reorganisation.
8. Do a rough budget for next year.
9. Spend the day with our new distributor.
10. Prepare a presentation for next month's supplier conference.

CASE STUDY: JENNIFER'S CHALLENGE

Jennifer supervises a team of six people but knows that they too have a heavy workload. She also has four peer supervisors. Unfortunately, one is off sick and two have complained that they will never get all their work finished before the holiday. Jennifer also knows that a temporary secretary is working on the same floor for the next week.

CASE STUDY: JENNIFER'S CHALLENGE

Jennifer's admin skills are average but she is quicker than most with the computer and is an excellent team communicator. This is ironic, since almost half her team's workload is in putting together a script for an information video to be released in the New Year to customers – but she is too busy to contribute to this.

Jennifer has never been able to delegate easily. She tends to think that she is faster than most people, even if she does make a few mistakes. However, she may have no option but to delegate if she wants to achieve her goals this year!

Questions to answer **before reading on**:

1. How should Jennifer plan her delegation approach?
2. Who could she approach and how might she win their support?
3. Which items could best wait?

CASE STUDY: JENNIFER'S CHALLENGE

Jennifer faces quite a challenge but delegation and plenty of collaboration are the keys here. Her first task should be some careful analysis and subsequent planning of her workload. Of the ten items on her list, at least two should not be delegated: Phil's appraisal and talking to the team about next year's reorganisation.

The other items all have potential to be delegated. A good approach is for her to estimate the time that each would take her. Given her average admin skills, the best tasks to delegate would be: proof reading and correcting the 80-page report (which the temporary secretary could do); planning the office relocation and the customer complaint exercise. Even designing the training course could be delegated, with a little extra help from her peers.

Although already very busy, her team would probably enjoy planning the office relocation and visiting the furniture supplier. They might even volunteer to work with her on the budget and to visit the new distributor. To eliminate some tasks altogether for now, the office supplier could send in catalogues and defer a visit, and the customer complaint analysis could wait until January.

COMMUNICATION & BRIEFING SKILLS

PRACTICAL DELEGATION SKILLS

In this and subsequent sections we are going to look at some of the practical skills that you will need in order to delegate well.

To give yourself the opportunity to succeed at delegation, you need to enlist the help of people you can trust to do a good job. However, this might be easier said than done.

The chances are that people to whom you would like to delegate are busy doing their own work and will not always take kindly to being asked to do more, especially if there is a strong culture of performance related pay and they feel that their regular work, on which their performance is being assessed, may suffer.

The challenge is to find ways to help them with their work in return, or to find other – sometimes less obvious – candidates who can do what you want or need capably.

FOLLOW A STEP BY STEP PLAN

Delegation should always follow a step by step plan, rather than be approached in a random fashion or unnecessarily rushed. The sequence doesn't need to be a fixed or standard process, but is likely to follow in some way the five stages that we outlined earlier.

By thinking through delegation in this ordered and sequential way, the delegator ensures that he or she has approached the whole process rigorously and thought about issues that might arise before briefing someone. Once this process becomes standard practice, it will save everyone a lot of time and energy by preventing missing steps or the errors that arise from poor preparation.

In the five stage list, the most important part is the preparation required for selecting the right task and the right person. Many people avoid spending any quality time on these first two steps and run into difficulties when they try to jump straight into briefing someone.

SELECTING INDIVIDUALS

As a general guide, when looking to find individuals to whom you can delegate, you want people who:

- Do what they say, in other words stick to their promises and commitments to others
- Display general competence, are good at what they do and don't make a fuss about it
- Are good team players, who support and help each other, not simply focusing upon their own agendas

The less obvious people are those you see as having potential to help: the quieter person who gets their work done without making a fuss; the person who shows interest in what others are doing, who asks intelligent questions, who demonstrates good listening skills.

POSSIBLE REACTIONS

When first discussing the possibility of delegating a task, the chances are that you'll get a whole range of reactions from the 'willing and able' to the *'I understand your need but I can't help'* approach. The more you prepare for these different kinds of responses, the more able you will be to paint a positive picture and to receive the help you require.

Your capacity to deal with reluctance to help will depend upon your:

- Ability to present an appealing case in the first place
- Powers of persuasion and asking for what you want
- Listening skills – usually this means keeping quiet more often!
- Capacity to see things from someone else's point of view
- Skill in thinking on your feet and offering alternatives where needed

All of this boils down to planning your style of engagement when first looking to brief someone.

BRIEFING STYLES

There are five commonly used briefing styles – shown below, with their pros and cons:

STYLE	PROS	CONS
FORMAL *'I have decided to appoint you to this acting position for the next two weeks.'*	• Helps people feel they have full authority to do the task • Lets others know who is in charge in a structured way	• May constrain the thinking on how the job should be done • May raise expectations of more permanent responsibility
INFORMAL *'Could you do this for me when you have the time and opportunity, please?'*	• Quick and easy method to use with people whose capabilities you know well • Good for smaller tasks with longer or not pressing deadlines	• Can be inappropriate for complex or detailed tasks with high levels of accountability • People may forget to do, or not complete, the task(s) assigned
COLLABORATIVE *'The whole team believes that you have the best skills for this task.'*	• Flattering and may raise commitment levels • Can engage individuals quickly in asking 'how to do it' questions	• Can put unnecessary pressure or influence on people who may not really want to perform the task • Can tend to single out individuals

BRIEFING STYLES

STYLE	PROS	CONS
PROBLEM FOCUSED *'I have a problem that needs your creative mind and approach – can you help me?'*	• Effectively invites ideas and sugge-stions on how to tackle the task • Generates questions about the problem and commitment to help solve it	• Can preclude input about why the issue or problem might exist in the first place • Can make delegates feel burdened unnecessarily when they have problems that are as great, if not greater
FULL EMPOWERMENT *'Could you take on this whole project and come up with new ideas on how we should proceed?'*	• Lots of scope for creativity • Can effectively create a climate for complete independence of action and approach	• Can fail to identify important milestones and measures of outcome success • May turn into abrogation without considerable care

Each of these styles will be appropriate in different circumstances or with different people. It is up to you to choose the right one for the right occasion.

NOT WHAT YOU SAY BUT HOW YOU SAY IT!

Whatever communication style you adopt, when delegating you are trying to persuade or influence someone to do what you want. Although we have outlined the different briefing styles, this is more about your personal communication style. Success depends both on what you say and how you say it.

People will not take kindly to starkly being told what to do without guidance or support, and being given no time to ask questions or clarify what might be expected.

For example, issuing a rushed directive to *'go to the weekly management meeting this afternoon and take minutes'*, without allowing time for questions, will create a situation in which the person's attitude to the task is negative and his or her contribution is likely to be sub-optimal. With a few seconds more, a friendlier demeanour and a statement such as *'Could you possibly go to the weekly management meeting this afternoon and take a few summary notes for me on what is discussed, so that we can meet afterwards to chat'*, you are more likely to achieve a positive attitude and result.

SELLING THE BENEFITS

As we have been suggesting, in order to obtain commitment you need to adopt a briefing approach that suits the individual and the circumstance. This involves selling or promoting the benefits of an idea or a suggestion in the first place and, with time, working towards a situation where you can give others the authority and commitment to do the job themselves.

Given that the average manager spends about 80% of the working day communicating, it would be fair to assume that we are all good at it. This is a dangerous assumption to make, however. You are better off taking the view that you can always achieve more if you invest more time in the communication process. This is usually best brought about by attentive listening and by keeping the whole communication open, warm and sincere.

CLEAR, CONCISE, COMPLETE

To be a good delegator you need to be as clear as you can – avoid vagueness and inaccuracy. This means being brief and to the point. Don't spend time giving reasons and excuses. Just say what you want and think in an honest and open fashion, using a pleasant and firm tone of voice.

You also need to be confident and persistent in explaining the whole of the task, especially when it is complex. Your requests are best delivered in a tone of voice that shows that you expect attention to be paid to you but that you are available to provide as much information as is needed.

Always avoid scolding, whining, apologising or rationalising why you are delegating the task. Behaviour like this will show that you are not sure whether what you are asking for is likely to be accepted, and so invites people to try to ignore you.

GIVING CLEAR INSTRUCTIONS

Here are some simple tips that may help you to give good clear instructions:

- It's important to say not only *what* you want done, but also *how, when, where, with whom*, and *why*. Perhaps the most important of all is *why*. Always give people a reason. Show how the task fits into the wider picture
- Don't presume that the individual has your perspective on things. You will have considerable experience, and have only come to your current level of knowledge through much learning
- Remember that everyone learns differently and sees differently. Don't presume that your way is the only way. If you are giving instructions, and it is obvious they are not being understood, try another tack
- Check to see that communication really has worked. Get the individual to repeat back to you – in their own words – what they understand the task to be. If there is any gap in understanding, fix it now
- Set up feedback and control mechanisms, so that the individual makes progress reports. Don't crowd, micro-manage or be a back-seat driver; show him or her the way, then get out of the way

DELEGATION STYLES

Earlier in this section, we talked about the different styles you can use when briefing someone. Although you *may* approach each opportunity to delegate in a different way, most people consistently utilise one approach or single style of delegating each time; one that may not always be appropriate to the situation.

Such style differences exist along a continuum. At one end of the continuum, a task or project may be delegated in name but not in practice. In other words, involvement in the work by the delegator can remain relatively high, and the person to whom the task has been delegated is left with very little room to do the job as he or she sees fit. This is called a **controlling** style.

At the other end of the continuum, a task is delegated with high levels of planning, care and involvement with the other person. This is called a **collaborative** style. In between these two extremes are what we call a **tentative** style and a **participative** style.

DELEGATION STYLES

QUESTIONNAIRE

In order to assess which delegation style you tend to adopt the most, what follows is a short questionnaire (adapted from a more in-depth online assessment). Your task is simply to review this list of 12 statements and identify the four that you think most reflect your general behaviour when it comes to delegating.

1. I like to look for individual strengths and delegate important tasks that I know will be challenging to the person concerned.
2. I talk to individuals about their relative skills and interests as a basis for discussion about future workload handling.
3. I like to delegate, but I worry about whether people have the skills and time to do the work well.
4. If a task I have delegated is likely to fall short of a target or to be late, I step in to help.
5. I give people the room to do a delegated task as they see fit, but stay around for advice if it is needed.

DELEGATION STYLES

QUESTIONNAIRE

6. I often ask people if they would like to be involved in some delegated tasks.
7. I occasionally get involved in a delegated task if I see a person does not have a lot of confidence.
8. I delegate small and relatively minor tasks from time to time.
9. I work with individuals to discover what they feel capable of handling.
10. I check up on people frequently when I have delegated a task or project.
11. I tend to delegate to people when the task is clearly defined and well within the individual's ability to handle it.
12. I tend to delegate to people as a last resort when I can't do a task or project myself.

DELEGATION STYLES

QUESTIONNAIRE: RESULTS

So how did you do?

In the assessment, questions 1, 5 and 9 relate to a **collaborative** delegation style. If you picked more of these questions than others, this is the style you seem to prefer.

Questions 2, 6 and 10 relate to a **participative** delegation style. If you picked more of these questions than others, this is the style you seem to prefer.

Questions 3, 7 and 11 relate to a **tentative** delegation style. If you picked more of these questions than others, this is the style you seem to prefer.

Questions 4, 8 and 12 relate to a **controlling** delegation style. If you picked more of these questions than others, this is the style you seem to prefer.

The next page gives you more information on the different styles.

CONTROLLING STYLE

So what does it mean to have a strong preference for one of these styles when delegating? The following descriptions briefly explain the basic characteristics of each of the four delegation styles:

Individuals with a **controlling** delegation style are likely to give tasks or projects to others on an occasional basis. However, when they do so, they often strongly supervise so that they can potentially better control the quality of the input effort and the amount of time that the work takes to complete.

The downside of this approach is that the supervision of work effort can be overdone. Individuals feel micro-managed and as if they are not fully trusted to perform the task or project alone.

TENTATIVE STYLE

Individuals with a **tentative** style are likely to be willing to delegate work more frequently but will have several reservations. These reservations may extend to doubts about the other person's experience, capability or work quality. Consequently, it takes longer to delegate a task, or only part of a task is actually offered up.

The downside of this approach is that the feelings of reservation are often visible for others to see. This does little for the confidence of the person asked to do the work, who may even question the value of starting the task at all.

PARTICIPATIVE STYLE

Individuals with a **participative** delegation style usually delegate work frequently, as a prime means to help individuals work in teams and experience different tasks, to which they may have had little or no previous exposure. People working in this style like to stay closely involved with the person to whom the work is delegated.

The downside of this approach is that not every delegated task lends itself to teamwork and the individual may not appreciate such close participation, having been asked to work on a delegated project.

COLLABORATIVE STYLE

Individuals with a **collaborative** delegation style are likely to make a much more careful assessment about the individuals who will benefit from delegated work and then offer tasks to each person on a selected basis. This will mean close collaboration with each individual in the early stages, to determine how much confidence he or she has in doing the task, and subsequently collaborating as much or as little as necessary.

The downside of this approach is that some individuals may feel (for good or bad) that they are always the ones selected for delegated tasks.

UNDERSTANDING YOUR STYLE

The benefit of knowing a little more about your preferred style is potentially to help you to develop, or further hone, your delegation skills in the future. The use of controlling, tentative or participative styles in particular is likely to be sub-optimal, at least to some extent.

A good delegator should consequently try to move along the continuum and aim to operate in a more collaborative way wherever possible. You can do this by thinking about how to make your preparation for delegation more effective, in terms of selecting the right tasks and choosing the most suitable people. Finally, try to work supportively and collaboratively with those entrusted with the work.

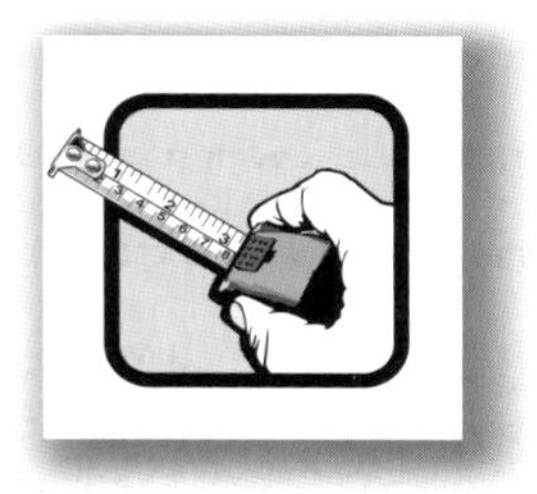

GOALS, OUTCOMES & MONITORING SYSTEMS

MEASURE PROGRESS

Delegation is the process of **smoothly** handing over responsibility to others. The timescales involved will depend on a variety of circumstances: the task, the person and the importance. It is therefore vital when delegating that you consider how you are going to measure progress.

Make sure that you do not cut short the time needed to discuss goals and targets. This will be the ultimate measure of whether or not a delegated task has been a success.

Checks and monitoring systems may involve a simple agreement about how often the delegator will be around to help and assist, how frequently the individual should report back on progress, and where extra help or assistance may be necessary to catch up.

GOALS FIT FOR PURPOSE

Successful completion of any delegated task requires a combination of knowledge, skills and attitudes. When assessing an individual's ability to take on a task, you can test their **knowledge** by asking what they know, and their **skills** by observing them in action.

There may be a shortfall between where people are now and where you want them to be. As a result, you should always look to set goals, targets and deadlines (as well as any necessary milestones along the way) that are commensurate with the person's capability. It is also important to ensure that the individual understands exactly what needs to be done.

Don't forget, delegation is about helping people achieve a goal to the required standard. This is something that they may not necessarily be able to do without help and assistance from you.

DELEGATION & SMART GOALS

Setting SMART goals (Specific, Measurable, Agreed, Realistic and Time-bound) will always help the person to whom you are delegating. The secret, however, is to ensure that the overall objective is pitched at a level that will stretch the person at least a little and be interesting and different, without being impossible to achieve.

Having set the targets, your job is only just beginning. Often, most of the support and assistance is needed in the early stages of doing a task. You can therefore help the person by providing the information, resources and time, and by being around if needed (avoiding any kind of abdication as soon as the task is delegated).

DELEGATION & SMARTER GOALS

A simple rule for delegation goes beyond SMART to SMARTER. It's a quick checklist for proper delegation. In addition to the SMART categories we add:

- Enjoyable
- Recorded

Some interpretations of the E in the SMARTER acronym use Exciting. However, although a high level of motivation often results when a person achieves, and receives recognition for, a particular delegated task – and this in itself can be exciting – it is not always possible in reality to ensure that all delegated work is truly 'exciting' for the recipient. More importantly, you should invest time and energy to talk in broad terms about **how** the task may be achieved, making sure that the individual has the best possible chance **to enjoy** the experience as they go along (with as much help from you as is required).

The R for Recorded is, of course, simply part of the monitoring process. The act of recording what has been delegated, to whom and by when, often helps both parties to be absolutely clear about what has been agreed.

MILESTONES FOR LARGER TASKS

In addition to goals and targets, you need to come to an agreement about the time to be taken and the key stages in the process. Milestones or markers are important to establish, as a way both of checking progress and giving individuals something to aim for.

Deciding on the overall acceptable timeframe for the tasks or project, and the appropriate milestones, should not be determined lightly or dictated on a one-sided basis. The best approach is to discuss this jointly, decide what is best and agree this clearly before the conversation ends. Once again, you need to find the right balance here – too much requirement for them to check with you becomes micro-management; too little and things might get out of control.

MINIMISING RISK

Delegation inevitably involves some possible additional risk. That is, you may actually increase the risk of some unwanted outcomes happening because, typically, the individual does not have your level of experience.

Rather than just ignore or accept these risks as inevitable, try to identify them and, based on your analysis, introduce a monitoring process to help manage these possible outcomes more effectively. This doesn't need to be an elaborate or complex affair, but should assist in making both parties feel that they are not too exposed (especially when the task or project is a large one).

MINIMISING RISK

EXAMPLE

If you were delegating the task of interviewing an external job applicant, you would run the risk that the person might fail to elicit key information, reject an acceptable applicant, or even discriminate unfairly in some of his or her questions.

The point is, once you have identified the risks, you can start to manage them together as part of the process.

In this instance, you would probably decide to discuss in advance the information you want to get, brief the individual on discriminatory questions to avoid, and ask him or her to talk to you about any applicants before rejecting them.

USING GOOD RISK CONTROLS

Appropriate control mechanisms are the best way to manage potential risk. Of course, the best control of all is to eliminate risk entirely, but we have already established that some risk is an inevitable accompaniment to delegation. The next best thing is to put in place risk minimisation or mitigation controls.

Risk mitigation control mechanisms might include:

- Checking with the individual a little more frequently and providing more support when they are undertaking higher risk tasks
- Asking the individual to refer concerns or queries to you when they are operating in entirely new areas
- Getting the individual to work with a colleague for higher risk tasks
- Setting a financial limit on spending to limit the impact of any mistake or error that may be made

In the final analysis, there is no substitute for discussing face-to-face the task to be undertaken and agreeing together the best risk management approach to take.

KEEP IN TOUCH

Especially for longer-term or more complex delegation tasks, it is essential to let the person know how they are doing, and whether they have achieved the aims or outcomes envisaged. If not, you should review with them why things did not go to plan, and deal with the problems. You must absorb the consequences of failure (and pass on the credit for success).

There are many warning signs that people are having problems. Keep an eye out for:

- Missed deadlines, targets or milestones (you may be just as guilty of this)
- Continual excuses: *'I've been so busy …'*
- Difficulty meeting up with them (never around when you go looking for them)
- The quality of the work being poor when you do get to see it
- Too many mistakes that you have to correct
- Reports from others that they are struggling

If you recognise any of these – and there will be others – then take notice and, more importantly, take action, as soon as you can.

HOW TO RESPOND TO PROBLEMS

The table below sets out several ways in which you can take action when problems arise, such as those on the previous page.

Missing deadlines	Get together and discuss. Try negotiating new deadlines and make sure you have a good monitoring system in place.
Making continual excuses	Find out the facts and the reasons behind the excuses. More importantly, what is the effect on the task? Remember, failure to meet agreed timescales could cause major problems later.
Being unavailable	Make a point of getting to see them at the start or the end of the day if necessary (they can't just slip away!)
Poor quality of work	Look to re-establish standards and expectations, as well as reasons why this is important.
Too many mistakes	Point out the mistakes sooner rather than later and make the implications clear. However, the secret is to find out why they are being made in the first place. To test understanding of the task get them to play back – in their own words – what you have asked them to do. Then jointly explore why there are problems.
Reports that they are struggling	Don't rely simply on hearsay. Get the facts and check them out for yourself.

The message from all of these is to act sooner rather than later.

MORE FORMAL MONITORING SYSTEMS

If the project is long and/or involved, you may want to use one or more of the following more formal monitoring systems (recognising the pros and cons of course):

MONITORING SYSTEM	MAIN PROS	MAIN CONS
Involvement in all written and email correspondence	Keeps you informed and in the communication loop	Signals a certain lack of trust
Receiving a regular written progress report	Encourages good organisation	Written information may not reveal everything that is happening
Daily/frequent update discussions	Immediate feedback	May encourage over-involvement or micro-management
Regular review meetings with all those involved	Emphasises teamwork	Lessens feelings of personal responsibility
An open-door policy	Good for showing support and empowerment	Individuals may not always use their initiative

MAINTAINING RESPONSIBILITY & ACCOUNTABILITY

The following examples of different levels of decision-making responsibility suggest that there is a progressive hierarchy of delegation that you can use. Tier 1 is the lowest level of delegated freedom (basically none), while tier 8 is the highest.

1. **'Wait to be told' or 'Do exactly what I say' or 'Follow these instructions.'**
   This is instruction. There is no real delegated freedom here.
2. **'Look into this and let me know the situation so that I can decide.'**
   Asks for investigation and analysis but no recommendation. The delegator retains responsibility for assessing options prior to making the decision.
3. **'Look into this and tell me the situation. We'll decide together.'**
   Encourages and enables the analysis and decision to be a shared process, which can be very helpful in coaching and development.
4. **'Tell me the situation and what help you need from me in assessing and handling it. Then we'll decide.'**
   Opens up the possibility of greater freedom for analysis and decision-making. Again, this level is helpful in growing and defining coaching and development relationships.

MAINTAINING RESPONSIBILITY & ACCOUNTABILITY

5. **'Give me your analysis of the situation (reasons, options, pros and cons) and your recommendation. I'll let you know whether you can go ahead.'** Asks for analysis and recommendation, but the delegator checks the thinking before deciding.
6. **'Decide and tell me your decision; wait for my go-ahead before proceeding.'** The other person is trusted to assess the situation and options, and is probably competent to decide and implement. For reasons of task importance, or competence, or externally changing factors, the delegator prefers to control the timing.
7. **'Decide and let me know your decision, then go ahead unless I say not to.'** This subtle increase in responsibility saves time. The default is now positive rather than negative. This is a very liberating change in delegated freedom.
8. **'Decide and take action – let me know what you did (and what happened).'** This level, as with each move up the scale, saves even more time. It also enables the delegator to follow up the effectiveness of the delegated responsibility, which is necessary when people are being managed from a distance or are more hands-off.

SUPPORT & COACHING

COACHING THROUGH DELEGATION

Delegation is an ideal opportunity to provide coaching for individuals.
This typically involves:

- Finding out what each person can do (which may take some on-going discussion)
- Agreeing some performance targets (both personal and team-based)
- Watching the person in action (to spot both strengths and development needs)
- Giving feedback and planning next steps (so that delegation is not just one-off)

With coaching you are jointly working out how best to approach a situation or problem. In so doing, you are sharing your experience of what works, as well as raising the performance of the other person. To be a skilled coach you need to be good at building rapport (being on the same wavelength), observing (and interpreting what's happening), asking questions, listening, giving feedback, helping people learn and developing trust.

ENCOURAGEMENT

Perhaps the greatest skill that you need when you are delegating a significant task or project and trying to coach someone, is the ability to encourage others to go beyond their current level of performance.

To encourage or motivate people successfully you may find it useful to:

- Share what you know about how the task could be done
- Invest quality time for the sake of the other person (failure to do so will clearly affect the result)
- Show the individual concerned that you have faith in his or her ability
- Accept that the credit for improvements or success goes to the other person but anything that goes wrong is your responsibility

It also helps if you enjoy working with people.

PUSH & PULL COACHING STRATEGIES

There are two basic approaches to choosing a coaching strategy when delegating. The **push** strategy is effective when you know exactly what to delegate or are clear about the solution to a problem. This a very direct coaching approach in which you:

- Set the scene, identify the problem or opportunity and make your proposal for the solution
- Invite reactions from the person to whom you wish to delegate
- Summarise the discussion and make sure that you understand each other
- Deal with any objections, either by persuasion or authority, depending upon whether you want commitment or compliance
- Agree the outcome – what is going to be done by when?

It's quite a powerful approach, the art being to avoid making the other person feel overwhelmed or rebellious. Only use it in situations where time is at a premium. Be clear and firm about your proposals, but also be approachable so that the other person can feel free to discuss them and raise any concerns.

PUSH & PULL COACHING STRATEGIES

You'll usually get a different reaction by adopting a **pull** strategy. This aims to achieve joint agreement on what to do, rather than rely on one person's authority. It's ideal for delegation when the other person's commitment is essential, and can best be achieved by:

- Stating your view of the problem or situation
- Clarifying how the other person sees the situation
- Debating what forward options seem to present themselves
- Looking for a best solution, using as many of the other person's ideas as possible, especially if commitment is important
- Reaching a joint agreement on what action to take

Both push and pull coaching are appropriate to use in the right circumstances, but you will generally find that a pull coaching approach is more motivating for the other person.

PULL COACHING STRATEGY

The **pull** strategy calls for a quite different set of skills from the **push**. Here, you need to let the other person know that you are trying to work together but give plenty of room for him or her to make their own contribution to the forward path. You therefore need to be supportive so that the other person is encouraged to make suggestions.

The most powerful thing you can do in such situations is to appeal to their imagination. Get them to picture how things could be in the future. Once they start to build an owned vision for the future they are likely to be much closer to being fully committed to the task in question.

The pull coaching approach significantly helps to develop the other person's ability to work out solutions to problems and make decisions. As such, it is ideal to use when delegating larger-scale projects in which there may be multiple acceptable solutions or outcomes.

RECOGNISING THE CONTRIBUTION

Whenever you delegate tasks of any kind, it's important that those involved can see some measure of success – or their progress – sooner rather than later. That in itself can be motivational and spur them on, particularly on larger or more complex projects.

Don't forget to be available at all times to offer help, assistance and recognition. Other people's success is a reflection of your own skills. If they fail at a job, then you should look at yourself, rather than seek to allocate blame. For this reason, it is vital that you maintain an open relationship with people. Keep an eye on the task or project that you have delegated, and offer a little encouragement now and again to boost confidence.

This may only be a quick *well done* or a one-line email but it can work wonders in helping to maintain an individual's overall momentum to finishing the delegated task well.

WAYS TO RECOGNISE EFFORT

Obviously, there are many ways to recognise and occasionally reward people's efforts, both while the delegated task is being undertaken and at the end. Here are a few ideas to try:

- Openly acknowledge hard work, commitment and effort when you see it. This is particularly important to encourage people who may lack confidence in their ability in a new task or at the early stages of a large project
- Take an informal interest in the task you have delegated by dropping by to see how things are going and offering direct encouragement on progress (even if the progress is actually only minor, in reality)
- Praise initiative, creativity or innovation wherever you see it
- On longer delegated tasks, write a note to the individual to congratulate them about a particular way they have chosen to tackle things
- Tell other team members about good achievements or praiseworthy efforts when they occur
- Thank people personally when the delegated task is complete

LEARNING FROM THE EXPERIENCE

KEEP IMPROVING

As you become more confident that delegation is a useful and beneficial process to engage in (perhaps having been reluctant in the past), it is worth working to improve your technique in every way you can.

One of the best ways to do this and lift your overall skills is to try always to learn from your delegation experiences (the ones that worked well and the ones that didn't), and adjust your approach for the next time. This might mean looking at how well you selected a person for a delegated task in the first place, how well you briefed him or her, the extent to which you were able to adjust your delegation style or the need to use better monitoring systems.

In all cases, trying continually to improve your own skills in small ways, every time, pays dividends.

LOOK FOR POTENTIAL

One of the most unfortunate side effects of the failure to delegate is the waste of human potential. Most organisations contain a wealth of unrecognised potential, but much of it stays unused because people are rarely given the chance to show what they can do, and to learn new things. People need new and different challenges in order to grow and learn; delegation presents many opportunities to provide those challenges. Looking for people's future potential is therefore a key area of focus when reflecting on your whole delegation approach.

One way to reflect on people's future potential is to start looking for possibilities for every individual in your team to do part of your job from time to time. Then find specific opportunities for this to occur by way of projects, special assignments and short-term step-up or cover roles as they arise.

This might sound a little risky – perhaps some people will be better at a task than you are – but in reality it helps both parties to grow.

LEARNING FROM THE EXPERIENCE

HARNESS ENTHUSIASM

Everyone gets stale doing the same thing day in, day out. Some people are happy in this environment, but a fair number are discontented and would relish the chance to try something new. They will consequently bring to the task higher levels of motivation, energy, enthusiasm and concentration, and the ability to bring fresh perspectives and new approaches to problem solving. Delegation generally gives the opportunity for all of these things to be expressed, and that's good news for the overall effectiveness of the organisation.

Of course, the advantages of regularly taking on delegated tasks are many and various for the individual(s) concerned. Picking up new skills and working in new areas helps to refresh people. They become multi-skilled, and gain a broader perspective of how the entire organisation works. New professional friendships give them wider communication networks, and may help to break down harmful dynamics.

FIND WAYS TO MOTIVATE & EMPOWER

Delegation increases people's sense of empowerment and motivation. The following are seen to be six key factors:

- **Skill variety** – the extent to which an individual has a variety of tasks to perform that extends his/her talents and skills
- **Task identity** – the extent to which a job role entails an individual completing a whole task, and not just a specialised aspect of it
- **Task significance** – the extent to which the individual's input to the whole enterprise is significant, and is perceived to be so by the worker
- **Autonomy** – the extent to which an individual has discretion and independence on task factors such as scheduling and quality control
- **Feedback** – the extent to which the individual gets clear information about his/her work output and performance
- **Career-path improvement** – the extent to which a job role expands so that the individual has better career and salary prospects

If delegation is done well, it should provide positive impacts in all six areas.

A DEVELOPMENTAL APPROACH

As we've mentioned throughout this book, opportunities for individuals to take on delegated tasks or projects are an excellent way in which to build job experience and even develop new skills for future career purposes.

For those individuals prepared to handle a difficult assignment, delegation provides the chance to provide the necessary training to get them up to speed. If people aren't quite ready yet, it is always possible to begin by delegating smaller chunks of a project before moving to tougher tasks. This means stretching people according to their capabilities and interests, and letting them taste success, then move them to the next level of responsibility. Even the slowest performer can pick up speed if a manager signals that they are trusted to take on the project and do a good job.

A DEVELOPMENTAL APPROACH

MINI CASE STUDY

To look at how delegation can be used as a coaching and development tool, read the mini case study below and, before turning the page, reflect on the question asked at the end.

Hannah felt that her group would benefit from a little teambuilding, and thought that she might bring in an external expert to facilitate a half-day session at the next team meeting. As Hannah thought about the five people in her team, however, she wondered whether delegation might provide some career growth.
Here are her notes:

John: *Great communicator and presenter*
Sally: *Intuitive and creative*
Rashid: *Very organised, good written work*
Erica: *Great team spirit, helps everyone else*
Brian: *Good project manager, always well-prepared*

Given her idea for the teambuilding meeting, what, in your opinion, should Hannah do?

A DEVELOPMENTAL APPROACH

MINI CASE STUDY

So how did you do?

Of course, Hannah has many options open to her, including getting help from external sources if she still thinks this would be valuable. With the skills within the group that she has identified, however, she seems to have lots of opportunities internally to put together a successful event. For instance she could:

1. Delegate to Brian the task of arranging the teambuilding session (the venue, the overall outline timing of the event), working with Sally.
2. Delegate to Sally the task of coming up with the creative structure, with ideas and input sessions that the team would benefit from.
3. Delegate to Erica the task of inviting everyone to the event and talking to individuals about what a great opportunity it could be.
4. Ask John to be the session facilitator.
5. Ask Rashid to synthesise all the input from the session and circulate notes and action plans after it.

This would play to each of their existing strengths. You might also like to reflect on what Hannah could do to stretch them a little further.

CAPTURING THE LEARNING

You should by now be convinced that delegation provides an excellent example of matching the demands of getting the job done with the business of providing opportunities for learning and development.

Having said that, it's important that a conscious attempt is made to capture any learning that arises from the successes and from those things that went less well.

Often what is learned is unacknowledged and unexplored. It is left to individuals to learn intuitively with no check on the relevance or quality of the learning. **Getting individuals to share what they have picked up, provides an opportunity for others to learn as well**. It is worth, therefore, putting a little time aside at the end of the delegated task to reflect and realistically appraise what went well and what could have been done differently (for future reference).

AREAS UNSUITABLE FOR DELEGATION

Some tasks and realms of activity are more suitable for delegation than others. The following are broad areas that are either hard to delegate or shouldn't be delegated at all in most situations (see also the onion diagram on page 40):

Leadership – overall leadership decision-making skills should always be retained, but it is possible to delegate the more control oriented aspects of leadership, such as monitoring performance and regular reporting on tasks or projects

Strategy – strategy is, usually, a long-term activity unsuited to the more short-term nature of delegation

Communication – parts of the communication process can be delegated but important communications are best retained

Measurement – the delegator will usually design and control the measurement system

Reward and recognition – the delegator should always be the one to reward and recognise an individual for a job well done

INVITING INPUT

If you can, look for feedback from every quarter, on a formal or informal basis, to make sure that your delegation approach is **fair**, **responsible** and **empowering** rather than **unmeasurable**, **burdening of others** or perceived as **abdicating too much**.

At its most straightforward, you can always ask an individual what they have learned from the experience and what they would do differently next time. Remember that you can ask this at every stage of the delegation process.

If the delegated task involves the individual in dealing with customers or suppliers, then you have a chance to ask for feedback from these third parties. In other words, what was it like on the receiving end? This is useful because it gives you another perspective.

KEY REVIEW QUESTIONS

Finally (and perhaps most importantly) you need to include your own ability as a delegator in the learning evaluation process. What did you learn about delegating to others?

- How good was your preparation and planning ... and why?
- How well did you explain what you wanted?
- What support did you have to give ... and why?
- Where were you anxious or concerned ... and why?
- What would you do differently next time ... and why?
- What were the major lessons for you from the whole experience?

Writing down the answers to these questions is a useful way of acknowledging that learning has taken place (from both sides), making it a conscious process for all concerned.

MOVING ON & IMPROVING

Perhaps by now you're feeling a little more willing to delegate than you ever thought possible – but why stop there? Delegation isn't a one-off event. To be effective, it should be built into your daily way of working.

Look at those everyday things that you tend to do out of habit, routine or simply because you enjoy doing them. Ask yourself:

- Do they need to be done in the first place?
- Do they need to be done by you?
- What jobs could you let others do and be responsible for?

PRACTICE MAKES PERFECT

In the final analysis, there is no prescriptive formula for delegation. Just like the whole process of empowering others, much of the success of the delegation process depends on the quality of the relationship between the delegator and those taking on the task(s) to be delegated. The higher the levels of trust and a feeling of genuine need (not a task 'dumping'), the more people are likely to perform well and a mutually satisfactory outcome will result.

For the most part, efforts to delegate efficiently and effectively require practice and a willingness to take a hard look at any shortfalls that arise on either side. Once done, an improvement strategy can be set in place to make the whole effort better the next time. Such improvements are usually best when incremental, or one step at a time, with an attitude that it is always possible to find a better way.

DELEGATION DO's & DON'Ts

To help wrap things up neatly, the list below represents a simple checklist rating of things to avoid when delegating a task:

Don't

- ✗ Be impatient and too hurried in trying to delegate
- ✗ Regard people around you as too inexperienced or incompetent
- ✗ Ask people to do things that you wouldn't do yourself
- ✗ Abrogate (instead of carefully delegate) your responsibilities
- ✗ Put people under unnecessary pressure when you have empowered them to act
- ✗ Take delegated tasks back without very good cause
- ✗ Blame people when you haven't briefed them properly or given them the necessary resources or authority to do the job
- ✗ Worry about people excelling at the delegated task – this is a major win for you, the person and the organisation as a whole

DELEGATION DO's & DON'Ts

We can't have a list of don'ts without a similar list of what you should do when delegating:

Do

- ✔ Ask others for help and assistance when you need it
- ✔ Communicate regularly with people around you about your tasks/goals
- ✔ Invite opinions or suggestions on how things might be done
- ✔ Follow a logical and ordered delegation sequence
- ✔ Communicate clearly in language that people will understand
- ✔ Adopt a range of different briefing/influencing styles for different people
- ✔ Indicate your belief in people's competence
- ✔ Take the blame for any failures but pass on the praise for any successes

THE DELEGATION CHARTER

Finally, the following is an easy to remember list, with the first letter of each statement spelling the word 'Delegate'.

The Delegation Charter

D oing it yourself or being a 'loner' is a poor option more often than you might think

E ffectiveness in terms of outcomes and not inputs is the key measure of your success

L ist all the jobs you face to see what can be delegated

E ngage others in conversations about helping you

G enerate people's interest and commitment

A sk people where they might need help from you

T rain and coach people in how to do the task(s)

E valuate progress along the way and don't abdicate your responsibility

LAST WORD

This book has suggested that effective delegation can be achieved through the deployment of a simple staged approach in which you:

- Start to appreciate or understand your own opportunities to delegate
- Prepare carefully
- Brief people clearly
- Maintain contact with people to whom you delegate
- Always learn from your experiences

This is not to say that delegation is easy to define or practise, and one can spend a lifetime trying to do it well. It is an essential technique, however, if you want to achieve all that you have to in today's busy world. In this sense, delegation is not an option but a necessary part of leading yourself and others to better things.

By following the guidance offered in this book, you should be better able to tackle the challenge.

USEFUL INFORMATION

REFERENCES

The following books provide useful reading if you wish to learn more.

If You Want It Done Right, You Don't Have to Do It Yourself! The Power of Effective Delegation, Donna M Genett, Quill Driver Books, 2003

Making Delegation Happen: A Simple and Effective Guide to Implementing Successful Delegation, Robert Burns, Allen & Unwin, 2002

Delegation Skills, Bruce Tepper, Irwin Professional, 1994

Successful Delegation, Bill Truby, Joann Truby, and William A. Newman, Truby Achievement Center, 2000

How to Delegate, Robert Heller and Tim Hindle, DK Publishing, 1999

The Agile Managers's Guide to Delegating Work, Joseph Straub, Velocity Publications, 1998

Effective Delegation, Chris Roebuck, AMACOM, 1999

About the Author

Dr. Jon Warner

Dr. Jon Warner operated as a senior professional manager, with over 25 years' experience in a number of major multi-national companies in the United Kingdom, Europe, the United States of America and Australia. This experience has included time as a senior staff manager in human resources and a number of line roles with responsibility for large groups of people. During the last 10 years Jon has been involved in broad ranging organisational consultancy and the pursuit of best-practice leadership. This consulting has taken him into a number of major organisations such as Mobil Oil, HSBC, BTR, Qantas, Barclays, United Energy, Air Products and Chemicals, Avon Products and Lloyds TSB. Jon Warner is also Managing Director of Team Publications Pty Limited, an international training and publishing company committed to bringing practical and fun-to-use learning material to the market.

Contact

UK: 5 The Hermitage, Portsmouth Road, Kingston-Upon-Thames, Surrey. Tel: 0208 546 4843
USA: 8939 Sepulveda Blvd, Suite 110-705, Los Angeles, California 90045. Tel: 310 430 8782
E-mail: Jon@OD-center.org

THE MANAGEMENT POCKETBOOK SERIES

Pocketbooks

360 Degree Feedback
Appraisals
Assertiveness
Balance Sheet
Business Planning
Business Writing
Call Centre Customer Care
Career Transition
Coaching
Communicator's
Competencies
Controlling Absenteeism
Creative Manager's
C.R.M.
Cross-cultural Business
Customer Service
Decision-making
Delegation
Developing People
Discipline
Diversity
E-commerce
Emotional Intelligence
Employment Law
Empowerment
Energy and Well-being
Facilitator's
Flexible Workplace
Handling Complaints
Icebreakers
Impact & Presence
Improving Efficiency
Improving Profitability
Induction
Influencing
International Trade
Interviewer's
I.T. Trainer's
Key Account Manager's
Leadership
Learner's
Manager's
Managing Budgets
Managing Cashflow
Managing Change
Managing Difficult Participants
Managing Recruitment
Managing Upwards
Managing Your Appraisal
Marketing
Meetings
Mentoring
Motivation
Negotiator's
Networking
NLP
Openers & Closers
People Manager's
Performance Management
Personal Success
Positive Mental Attitude
Presentations
Problem Behaviour
Problem Solving
Project Management
Psychometric Testing
Resolving Conflict
Reward
Sales Excellence
Salesperson's
Self-managed Development
Starting In Management
Strategy
Stress
Succeeding at Interviews
Talent Management
Teambuilding Activities
Teamworking
Telephone Skills
Telesales
Thinker's
Time Management
Trainer Standards
Trainer's
Training Evaluation
Training Needs Analysis
Virtual Teams
Vocal Skills
Workplace Politics

Pocketsquares

Great Training Robbery

Pocketfiles

Trainer's Blue Pocketfile of Ready-to-use Activities

Trainer's Green Pocketfile of Ready-to-use Activities

Trainer's Red Pocketfile of Ready-to-use Activities

21.04.08

ORDER FORM

Your details

Name ______________________

Position ______________________

Company ______________________

Address ______________________

____

____

Telephone ______________________

Fax ______________________

E-mail ______________________

VAT No. (EC companies) ______________________

Your Order Ref ______________________

Please send me:

			No. copies
The	Delegation	Pocketbook	
The		Pocketbook	
The		Pocketbook	
The		Pocketbook	

Order by Post

MANAGEMENT POCKETBOOKS LTD

LAUREL HOUSE, STATION APPROACH,
ALRESFORD, HAMPSHIRE SO24 9JH UK

MANAGEMENT POCKETBOOKS

Order by Phone, Fax or Internet

Telephone: +44 (0)1962 735573
Facsimile: +44 (0)1962 733637
E-mail: sales@pocketbook.co.uk
Web: www.pocketbook.co.uk

Customers in USA should contact:

Management Pocketbooks
2427 Bond Street, University Park, IL 60466
Telephone: 866 620 6944 Facsimile: 708 534 7803
E-mail: mp.orders@ware-pak.com
Web: www.managementpocketbooks.com